"This is an intricate, muscular, startlingly powerful collection, one that amazes by image and statement, by its shaped whole, and by the sheer scope of its poetic observation. Kaminsky is truly a descendant of Odysseus, after whom his birth city was named. . . . Inventiveness of language, the investigative passion, praises, lamentation, and a proper sense of the ridiculous are omnipresent. . . . This book is a breathtaking debut."
 —Jane Hirshfield, *Ploughshares*

"A superb and vigorous imagination, a poetic talent of rare and beautiful proportions, whose work is surely destined to be widely and enthusiastically noticed and applauded. This is the start of a brilliant career."
 —Anthony Hecht

"With his magical style in English, poems in *Dancing in Odessa* seem like a literary counterpart to Chagall in which laws of gravity have been suspended and colors reassigned, but only to make everyday reality that much more indelible. . . . Kaminsky's imagination is so transformative that we respond with equal measures of grief and exhilaration."
 —American Academy of Arts and Letters'
 Citation for the Addison M. Metcalf Award

"Like Joseph Brodsky before him, Kaminsky is a terrifyingly good poet . . . who, having adopted English, has come to put us native speakers to shame. . . . It seemed to take about five minutes to read this book, and when I began again, I reached the end before I was ready. That's how compulsive, how propulsive it is to read."
 —John Timpane, *The Philadelphia Inquirer*

Winners of The Dorset Prize

Ice, Mouth, Song by Rachel Contreni Flynn
Selected by Stephen Dunn

Red Summer by Amaud Jamaul Johnson
Selected by Ray Gonzalez

Dancing in Odessa by Ilya Kaminsky
Selected by Eleanor Wilner

Dismal Rock by Davis McCombs
Selected by Linda Gregerson

Biogeography by Sandra Meek
Selected by the Tupelo Press Editors

Archicembalo by G. C. Waldrep
Selected by C. D. Wright

Severance Songs by Joshua Corey
Selected by Ilya Kaminsky

After Urgency by Rusty Morrison
Selected by Jane Hirshfield

Dancing In Odessa

Ilya Kaminsky

TUPELO PRESS

North Adams, Massachussets

Dancing in Odessa.
Copyright 2004 Ilya Kaminsky. All rights reserved.
ISBN: 978-1-932195-12-5
Library of Congress Control Number: 2003115523

Cover and text designed by Bill Kuch, WK Graphic Design.

First paperback edition: 2004.

Tupelo Press
P.O. Box 1767, North Adams, Massachusetts 01247
Telephone: (413) 664–9611 / Fax: (413) 664–9711
editor@tupelopress.org / www.tupelopress.org

Tupelo Press is an award-winning independent literary press that
publishes fine fiction, non-fiction, and poetry in books that are a
joy to hold as well as read. Tupelo Press is a registered 501(c)3 non-
profit organization, and we rely on public support to carry out our
mission of publishing extraordinary work that may be outside the
realm of the large commercial publishers. Financial donations are
welcome and are tax deductible.

for my family

Мне голос был

CONTENTS

Author's Prayer

If I speak for the dead, I must leave
this animal of my body,

I must write the same poem over and over,
for an empty page is the white flag of their surrender.

If I speak for them, I must walk on the edge
of myself, I must live as a blind man

who runs through rooms without
touching the furniture.

Yes, I live. I can cross the streets asking "What year is it?"
I can dance in my sleep and laugh

in front of the mirror.
Even sleep is a prayer, Lord,

I will praise your madness, and
in a language not mine, speak

of music that wakes us, music
in which we move. For whatever I say

is a kind of petition, and the darkest
days must I praise.

Dancing in Odessa

Dancing in Odessa

In a city ruled jointly by doves and crows, doves covered the main district, and crows the market. A deaf boy counted how many birds there were in his neighbor's backyard, producing a four-digit number. He dialed the number and confessed his love to the voice on the line.

My secret: at the age of four I became deaf. When I lost my hearing, I began to see voices. On a crowded trolley, a one-armed man said that my life would be mysteriously linked to the history of my country. Yet my country cannot be found, its citizens meet in a dream to conduct elections. He did not describe their faces, only a few names: Roland, Aladdin, Sinbad.

In Praise of Laughter

Where days bend and straighten
in a city that belongs to no nation
but all the nations of wind,

she spoke the speech of poplar trees—
her ears trembling as she spoke, my Aunt Rose
composed odes to barbershops, drugstores.

Her soul walking on two feet, the soul or no soul, a child's allowance,
she loved street musicians and knew
that my grandfather composed lectures on the supply

and demand of clouds in our country:
the State declared him an enemy of the people.
He ran after a train with tomatoes in his coat

and danced naked on the table in front of our house—
he was shot, and my grandmother raped
by the public prosecutor, who stuck his pen in her vagina,

the pen which signed people off for twenty years.
But in the secret history of anger—*one man's silence
lives in the bodies of others*—as we dance to keep from falling,

between the doctor and the prosecutor:
my family, the people of Odessa,
women with huge breasts, old men naive and childlike,

all our words, heaps of burning feathers
that rise and rise with each retelling.

Maestro

What is memory? what makes a body glow:
an apple orchard in Moldova and the school is bombed

when the schools are bombed, sadness is forbidden
—I write this now and I feel my body's weight:

the screaming girls, 347 voices
in the story of a doctor saving them, his hands

trapped under a wall, his granddaughter dying nearby—
she whispers *I don't want to die, I have eaten such apples.*

He touches her mouth as a blind man reading lips
and yells *Shut up! I am near the window, I*

am asking for help! speaking,
he cannot stop speaking, in the dark:

of Brahms, Chopin he speaks to them to calm them.
A doctor, yes, whatever window

framed his life, outside: tomatoes grew, clouds passed and we
once lived. A doctor with a tattoo of a parrot on his trapped arm,

seeing his granddaughter's cheekbones
no longer her cheekbones, with surgical precision

stitches suffering and grace:
two days pass, he shouts

in his window (there is no window) when rescue
approaches, he speaks of Chopin, Chopin.

They cut off his hands, nurses say he is "doing OK"
—in my dream: he stands, feeding bread to pigeons, surrounded

by pigeons, birds on his head, his shoulder,
he shouts *You don't understand a thing!*

he is breathing himself to sleep, the city sleeps,
there is no such city.

Aunt Rose

In a soldier's uniform, in wooden shoes, she danced
at either end of day, my Aunt Rose.
Her husband rescued a pregnant woman

from the burning house—he heard laughter,
each day's own little artillery—in that fire
he burnt his genitals. My Aunt Rose

took other people's children—she clicked her tongue as they cried
and August pulled curtains evening after evening.
I saw her, chalk between her fingers,

she wrote lessons on an empty blackboard,
her hand moved and the board remained empty.
We lived in a city by the sea but there was

another city at the bottom of the sea
and only local children believed in its existence.
She believed them. She hung her husband's

picture on a wall in her apartment. Each month
on a different wall. I now see her with that picture, hammer
in her left hand, nail in her mouth.

From her mouth, a smell of wild garlic—
she moves toward me in her pajamas
arguing with me and with herself.

The evenings are my evidence, this evening
in which she dips her hands up to her elbows,
the evening is asleep inside her shoulder—her shoulder

rounded by sleep.

My Mother's Tango

I see her windows open in the rain, laundry in the windows—
she rides a wild pony for my birthday,
a white pony on the seventh floor.

"And where will we keep it?" "On the balcony!"
the pony neighing on the balcony for nine weeks.
At the center of my life: my mother dances,

yes here, as in childhood, my mother
asks to describe the stages of my happiness—
she speaks of soups, she is of their telling:

between the regiments of saucers and towels,
she moves so fast—she is motionless,
opening and closing doors.

But what was happiness? A pony on the balcony!
My mother's past, a cloak she wore on her shoulder.
I draw an axis through the afternoon

to see her, sixty, courting a foreign language—
young, not young—my mother
gallops a pony on the seventh floor.

She becomes a stranger and acts herself, opens
what is shut, shuts what is open.

American Tourist

In a city made of seaweed we danced on a rooftop, my hands
under her breasts. Subtracting
day from day, I add this woman's ankles

to my days of atonement, her lower lip, the formal bones of her face.
We were making love all evening—
I told her stories, their rituals of rain: happiness

is money, yes, but only the smallest coins.
She asked me to pray, to bow
towards Jerusalem. We bowed to the left, I saw

two bakeries, a shoe store; the smell of hay,
smell of horses and hay. *When Moses*
broke the sacred tablets on Sinai, the rich

picked the pieces carved with:
"adultery" and "kill" and "theft,"
the poor got only "No" "No" "No."

I kissed the back of her neck, an elbow,
this woman whose forgetting is a plot against forgetting,
naked in her galoshes she waltzed

and even her cat waltzed.
She said: "All that is musical in us is memory"—
but I did not know English, I danced

sitting down, she straightened
and bent and straightened, a tremble of music
a tremble in her hand.

Dancing in Odessa

We lived north of the future, days opened
letters with a child's signature, a raspberry, a page of sky.

My grandmother threw tomatoes
from her balcony, she pulled imagination like a blanket
over my head. I painted
my mother's face. She understood
loneliness, hid the dead in the earth like partisans.

The night undressed us (I counted
its pulse) my mother danced, she filled the past
with peaches, casseroles. At this, my doctor laughed, his granddaughter
touched my eyelid—I kissed

the back of her knee. The city trembled,
a ghost-ship setting sail.
And my classmate invented twenty names for Jew.
He was an angel, he had no name,
we wrestled, yes. My grandfathers fought

the German tanks on tractors, I kept a suitcase full
of Brodsky's poems. The city trembled,
a ghost-ship setting sail.
At night, I woke to whisper: yes, we lived.
We lived, yes, don't say it was a dream.

At the local factory, my father
took a handful of snow, put it in my mouth.
The sun began a routine narration,
whitening their bodies: mother, father dancing, moving
as the darkness spoke behind them.
It was April. The sun washed the balconies, April.

I retell the story the light etches
into my hand: *Little book, go to the city without me.*

Musica Humana

[an elegy for Osip Mandelstam]

[A modern Orpheus: sent to hell, he never returned, while his widow
searched across one sixth of the earth's surface, clutching the saucepan with
his songs rolled up inside, memorizing them by night in case they were
found by Furies with a search warrant.]

While there is still some light on the page,
he escapes in a stranger's coat with his wife.
And the cloth smells of sweat;
a dog runs after them
licking the earth where they walked and sat.

In the kitchen, on a stairwell, above the toilet,
he will show her the way to silence,
they will leave the radio talking to itself.
Making love, they turn off the lights
but the neighbor has binoculars
and he watches, dust settling on his lids.

It is the 1930s: Petersburg is a frozen ship.
The cathedrals, cafés, down Nevski Prospect
they move, as the New State
sticks its pins into them.

[In Crimia, he gathered together rich 'liberals' and said to them strictly: On Judgment Day, if you are asked whether you understood the poet Osip Mandelstam; say no. Have you fed him? — You must answer yes.]

I am reading aloud the book of my life on earth
and confess, I loved grapefruit.
In a kitchen: sausages; tasting vodka,
the men raise their cups.
A boy in a white shirt, I dip my finger
into sweetness. Mother washes
behind my ears. And we speak of everything
that does not come true,
which is to say: it was August.
August! the light in the trees, full of fury. August
filling hands with language that tastes like smoke.
Now, memory, pour some beer,
salt the rim of the glass; you
who are writing me, have what you want:
a golden coin, my tongue to put it under.

(The younger brother of a cloud,
he walks unshaven in dark-green pants.
In cathedrals: he falls on his knees, praying HAPPINESS!
His words on the floor are the skeletons of dead birds.)

I've loved, yes. Washed my hands. Spoke
of loyalty to the earth. Now death,
a loverboy, counts my fingers.

I escape and am caught, escape again
and am caught, escape

and am caught: in this song,
the singer is a clay figure,

poetry is the self—I resist
the self. Elsewhere:

St. Petersburg stands
like a lost youth

whose churches, ships, and guillotines
accelerate our lives.

[In summer 1924 Osip Mandelstam brought his young wife to St. Petersburg.
Nadezhda was what the French call *laide mais charmante.* An eccentric? Of course
he was. He threw a student down the staircase for complaining he wasn't published,
Osip shouting: Was Sappho? Was Jesus Christ?]

Poet is a voice, I say, like Icarus,
whispering to himself as he falls.

Yes, my life as a broken branch in the wind
hits the Northern ground.
I am writing now a history of snow,
the lamplight bathing the ships
that sail across the page.

But on certain afternoons
the Republic of Psalms opens up
and I grow frightened that I haven't lived, died, not enough
to scratch this ecstasy into vowels, hear
splashes of clear, biblical speech.

I read Plato, Augustine, the loneliness of their syllables
while Icarus keeps falling.
And I read Akhmatova, her rich weight binds me to the earth,
the nut trees on a terrace breathing
the dry air, the daylight.

Yes, I lived. The State hung me up by the feet, I saw
St. Petersburg's daughters, swans,
I learned the grammar of gulls' array
and found myself for good
down Pushkin Street, while memory
sat in the corner, erasing me with a sponge.

I've made mistakes, yes: in bed
I compared government
to my girlfriend.
Government! An arrogant barber's hand
shaving off the skin.
All of us dancing happily around him.

[He sat on the edge of his chair and dreamt aloud of good dinners. He composed his
poems not at his desk but in the streets of St. Petersburg; he adored the image of the
rooster tearing apart the night under the walls of Acropolis with his song. Locked up
in the cell, he was banging on the door: "You have got to let me out, I wasn't made
for prison."]

Once or twice in his life, a man
is peeled like apples.

What's left is a voice
that splits his being

down to the center.
We see: obscenity, fright, mud

but there is joy of shape, there is
always
more than one silence.

—between here and Nevski Prospect,
the years, birdlike, stretch,—

Pray for this man
who lived on bread and tomatoes

while dogs recited his poetry
in each street.

Yes, count "march," "july"
weave them together with a thread –

it's time, Lord,
press these words against your silence.

❖

—the story is told of a man who escapes
and is captured

into the prose of evenings:
after making love, he sits up

on a kitchen floor, eyes wide open,
speaks of the Lord's emptiness

in whose image we are made.
*—he is out of work—*among silverware

and dirt he is kissing
his wife's neck so the skin of her belly tightens.

One would think of a boy laying
syllables with his tongue

onto a woman's skin: those are lines
sewn entirely of silence.

[Nadezhda looks up from the page and speaks: Osip, Akhmatova and I were standing together when suddenly Mandelstam melted with joy: several little girls ran past us, imagining themselves to be horses. The first one stopped, impatiently asking: "Where is the last horsy?" I grabbed Mandelstam by his hand to prevent him from joining; and Akhmatova, too, sensing danger, whispered: "Do not run away from us, you are our last horsy."]

—as I die, I walk barefoot across my country,
here winter builds the strongest
solitude, tractors break into centaurs
and gallop through plain speech:
I am twenty-three, we live in a cocoon,
the butterflies are mating.
Osip puts his fingers into fire; he
gets up early, walking around
in his sandals. Writes slowly. Prayers
fall into the room. Moths
are watching him from the window. As his tongue
passes over my skin, I see
his face from underneath,
its aching clarity
—thus Nadezhda speaks,
standing in an orange light,
her hands are quiet, talking
to themselves:
O God of Abraham, of Isaak and of Jacob
on your scale of Good and Evil,
put a plate of warm food.

❖

When my husband returned
from Voronezh, in his mouth
he hid a silver spoon—

in his dreams,
down Nevski Prospect, the dictator ran
like a wolf after his past,
a wolf with sleep in its eyes.

He believed in the human being. Could not
cure himself
of Petersburg. He recited by heart
phone numbers
of the dead.

O what he told in a low voice!—
the unspoken words became traces of islands.
When he slapped
Tolstoy in the face, it was good.

When they took my husband, each word
disappeared in a book.
They watched him
as he spoke: the vowels had teeth-marks.

And they said: *You must leave him alone*
for already behind his back
the stones circle all by themselves and fall.

[Osip had thick eyelashes, to the middle of his cheeks. We were walking along Prehistenka St., what we were talking about I don't remember. We turned onto Gogol Boulevard, and Osip said, "I am ready for death." At his arrest they were searching for poems, all over the floor. We sat in one room. On the other side of the wall, at a neighbor's, a Hawaiian guitar was playing. In my presence the investigator found "The Wolf" and showed it to Osip. He nodded slightly. Taking his leave, he kissed me. He was led away at 7A.M.]

At the end of each vision, Mandelstam
stands with a clod of earth, throwing
bits at the passers-by. You will recognize him, Lord:
—he hated Tsarskoe Selo,
told Mayakovski: "stop reading your verse, you are not
a Rumanian orchestra."
What harmony was? It raveled
and unraveled; Nadezhda said the snow fell inside her,
she heard the voice of young chickens all over her flesh.

Nadezhda, her Yes and No are difficult
to tell apart. She dances, a skirt tucked between her thighs
and the light is strengthening.
In each room's
four corners: he is making love to her earlobes, brows,
weaving days into knots.
He is traveling across her kitchen, touching furniture,
a small propeller in his head

turning as he speaks. Outside,
a boy pissing against the tree, a beggar
cursing at his cat—that summer 1938—
the walls were hot, the sun beat
against the city's slabs
'the city that loved to say *yes* to the powerful.'
At the end of each vision, he rubbed her feet with milk.
She opened her body, lay on his stomach.
We will meet in Petersburg, he said,
we have buried the sun there.

Musica Humana

His name was Osip but, either jokingly or in disguise, we called him Ovid. As the story goes, Ovid was a rose thief. He stole dozens of roses from the public parks at night, hiding them in his coat, then selling them at the train station in the morning. Ovid became famous when he stole the Governor's coat, and then sold it to the city's Chief Judge. While at the Judge's house, he stole a horse and went back to sell it to the Governor, mentioning that he saw the Judge wearing the stolen coat. The Governor saddled the stolen horse, galloping to its rightful owner to claim his own precious possession. As for Ovid, he moved to Argentina and became a cook. While soups overheated in a pot engraved with the word "obsession," he sang himself to sleep between the stove and the table:

"Cold Mint-Cucumber Soup"

2 tablespoons butter	Melt butter in a skillet with gar-
1 cup plain yogurt	lic, onion, cucumber; cook until
1 onion (chopped)	soft. Stir in stock. Blend, bring to
1 garlic clove	boil, puree. Blend in mint, chill.
3 cucumbers (sliced)	Before serving, stir in yogurt.
2 tablespoons rice flour	Mix.
2 cups chicken stock	
2 tablespoons fresh mint (chopped)	
Salt and pepper.	

"I will tell you a story," Ovid would say. I would shake my head, no thank you. "Ah, a romantic boy with a barefoot heart! Never have you been buried in the earth or savored the delicious meat of sacrifice! Listen to a story—

When, in his fifties, my uncle got sick, his two brothers went around the street with a "list of days." They asked the neighbors to give him a day or two of their own lives and to sign their names next to it. When they asked Natalia, a young girl next door who was secretly in love with him, she wrote: "I am giving you all my remaining life," and signed. Even his brothers tried to talk her out of it. They argued, voiced reasons: she would not listen. "All my remaining life," she said. "That is my wish."

The next morning, my uncle was up with a smile on his face while the girl's body was found at midday breathless in her own sweaty bed. The winter passed and then another winter. One by one the man's friends began to die, he buried his own brothers. He abhorred his existence. Every Sunday we saw him at the market, trying the fruits with his thumb, buying a peach or a pear, muttering to himself. He only spoke to children. One night, he said, it seemed as if he heard a distant music. Amazed, he understood—it was the day of Natalia's wedding, a choir in which she did not have a chance to sing. A year later, reading the Talmud, he stopped in the middle of a page, hearing a child's cry. Lord, he whispered, her baby is due today—a happiness she will never know. Her life, hour after hour, steamed before him. He heard music once more, wondering if it was her second marriage or her own daughter's early wedding. How many times he woke at night asking God to grant him death; but he lived. We saw him, each Sunday morning, at the market, buying fruit, counting the singles carefully. Once, in July, getting coins from his pocket to pay for a plum he began, violently, to rub his chest. He sat down on the pavement, whispering that he suddenly heard someone's sickening scream. We understood.

A Toast

If you will it, it is no dream.
                                    —Theodore Herzl

October: grapes hung like the fists of a girl
gassed in her prayer. *Memory,*
I whisper, *stay awake.*

In my veins
long syllables tighten their ropes, rains come
right out of the eighteenth century
Yiddish or a darker language in which imagination
is the only word.

Imagination! a young girl dancing polka,
unafraid, betrayed by the Lord's death
(or his hiding under the bed when the Messiah
was postponed).

In my country, evenings bring the rain water, turning
poplars bronze in a light that sparkles on these pages
where I, my fathers,
unable to describe your dreams, drink
my silence from a cup.

Natalia

Natalia

Her shoulder: an ode to an evening, such ambitions.

I promise I will teach her to ride horses, we will go to Mexico, Angola, Australia. I want her to imagine our scandalous days in Odessa when we will open a small sweets shop—except for her lovers and my neighbors (who steal milk chocolate by handfuls) we will have no customers. In an empty store, dancing among stands with sugared walnuts, dried carnations, boxes upon boxes of mints and cherries dipped in honey, we will whisper to each other our truest stories.

The back of her knee: a blessed territory, I keep my wishes there.

As I open the Tristia, evening spreads its nets
and a woman I love runs from a parking lot.
"You will run away," she says, "I already
see it: a train station, a slippery floor, a seat."

I tell her to leave me alone, inside my childhood
where men carry flags across the street.
And they tell her: leave us alone,
as if the power were given to them, but it is not given.

She attacks with passion, lifts her hand
and puts it in my hair. On my right side I hide a scar,
she passes over it with her tongue
and falls asleep with my nipple in her mouth.

But Natalia, beside me, turns the pages,
what happened and did not happen
must speak and sing by turns.
My chronicler, Natalia, I offer you two cups of air
in which you dip your little finger, lick it dry.

———————————————————————

This poem begins: "Late January, the darkness is handwritten onto trees."
As I speak of her, she sits at the mirror, combing her hair. From her hair the
water pours, the leaves fall. I undress her, my tongue passing over her skin.
"Potatoes!" she tells me, "I smell like potatoes!" and I touch her lips with
my fingers.

On the night I met her, the Rabbi sang and sighed,
god's lips on his brow, Torah in his arms.
—I unfastened her stockings, worried

that I have stopped worrying.
She slept in my bed—I slept on a chair,
she slept on a chair—I slept in the kitchen,

she left her slippers in my shower, in my Torah,
her slippers in each sentence I spoke.
I said: those I love—die, grow old, are born.

But I love the stubbornness of her bedclothes!
I bite them, taste bedclothes   —
the sweet mechanism of pillows and covers.

A serious woman, she danced
without a shirt, covering what she could.
We lay together on Yom Kippur, chosen by a wrong God,

the people of a book, broken by a book.

———————————————————————

I am going to stop this, I am going to stop quoting poems in my mind. She liked that. She carried banners protesting banners. Each night, she gave me beer and stuffed peppers. On a tape—she spoke and spoke and spoke. One button made her still. But her speech raised to my shoulders, my brows.

"Let me kiss you inside your elbow,
Natalia, sister of the careful"
—he spoke of gratitude, his fingers

trembling as he spoke.
She unfastened two buttons of his trousers—
to learn two languages:

one for ankles, and one for remembering.
Or maybe she thought it was bad luck
to have a dressed man in the house.

With an eyebrow pencil, she painted
his mustache: it made her
want to touch him and she didn't.

She opened her robe and
closed it, opened and closed it again,
she whispered: *come here, nervous*—

he followed her on his tiptoes.

"I don't need a synagogue," you said, "I can pray inside my body." You slept
without covering yourself. I couldn't tell departure from arrival. You spoke
inside my twice averted words—you yelled when you opened the doors, and
opened each door in silence.

    Someone else is on this page, writing. I attempt to move my fingers
faster than she.

We fell in love and eight years passed.
Eight years. Carefully, I dissect this number:
we've lived with three cats in five cities,

learning how a man ages invisibly.
Eight years! Eight! —I chilled lemon vodka, and we kissed
on the floor, among the peels of lemons.

And each night, looking up, we saw ourselves:
a man and a woman, whispering *Lord*,
one word the soul destroys to make clear.

How magical it is to live! it rained at the market,
with my fingers, she tapped out her iambics
on the back of our largest casserole,

and we sang, *Sweet dollars,*
why aren't you in my pockets?

(And suddenly) the joy of days entered me. She only danced under apricot
trees in a public park, a curious woman in spectacles whose ambition was
limited to apricot trees. I wrote: "Hold fast, my heart, I want to play a fool,
I want to rub each day's dusty coin." She laughed as she read this, I read over
her shoulder. I set my evening clock to the rhythm of her voice.

Envoi

You will die on a boat from Yalta to Odessa.

—a fortune teller, 1992

What ties me to this earth? In Massachusetts,
the birds force themselves into my lines—
the sea repeats itself, repeats, repeats.

I bless the boat from Yalta to Odessa
and bless each passenger, his bones, his genitals,
bless the sky inside his body,
the sky my medicine, the sky my country.

I bless the continent of gulls, the argument of their order.
The wind, my master
insists on the joy of poplars, swallows,—

bless one woman's brows, her lips
and their salt, bless the roundness
of her shoulder. Her face, a lantern
by which I live my life.

You can find us, Lord, she is a woman dancing with her eyes closed
and I am a man arguing with this woman
among nightstands and tables and chairs.

Lord, give us what you have already given.

Traveling Musicians

Traveling Musicians

In the beginning was the sea—we heard the surf in our breathing, certain that we carried seawater in our veins.

A city famous for its drunk tailors, huge mausoleums of rabbis, horse owners and horse thieves, and most of all, for its stuffed and baked fish. In Odessa, language always involved gestures—it was impossible to ask someone for directions if their hands were busy. I did ask once: a man was holding two huge watermelons, one in each arm. But as I asked more questions, his face grew red and ah! one watermelon fell on the ground as he attempted to gesticulate through the conversation. He was not disappointed, a man of fifty staring at the juicy watermelon meat right there on the sidewalk. He laughed like the most serious child I ever knew, telling me the story about the country where everyone was deaf.

A Farewell To Friends

after Nikolai Zabolotsky

Yes, each man is a tower of birds, I write my friends
into earth, into earth, into earth.

Here, with lantern in hand,
a beetle-man greets his acquaintances.

You stand in white hats, long jackets,
with notebooks of poems,

you have for sisters wild carnations,
nipples of lilacs, splinters and chickens.

Go now, I write as the pages turn
to the shuffle of your steps across the room.

Paul Celan

He writes towards your mouth
with his fingers.

In the lamplight he sees mud, wind bitten trees,
he sees grass still surviving this hour, page

stern as a burnt field:
Light was. Salvation

he whispers. The words leave the taste of soil
on his lips.

Paul Celan

As a youth, he worked in a factory, though everyone said he looked more like a professor of classical languages than a factory worker.

He was a beautiful man with a slender body that moved with a mixture of grace and sharp geometrical precision. His face had an imprint of laugher on it, as if no other emotion ever touched his skin. Even in his fifties, the nineteen-year-old girls winked at him in trains or trolley-busses, asking for his phone number.

Seven years after his death, I saw Celan in his old robe dancing alone in his bedroom, humming step over step. He did not mind being a character in my stories in a language he never learned. That night, I saw him sitting on a rooftop, searching for Venus, reciting Brodsky to himself. He asked if his past existed at all.

Elegy for Joseph Brodsky

In plain speech, for the sweetness
between the lines is no longer important,
what you call immigration I call suicide.
I am sending, behind the punctuation,
unfurling nights of New York, avenues
slipping into Cyrillic—
winter coils words, throws snow on a wind.
You, in the middle of an unwritten sentence, stop,
exile to a place further than silence.

❖

I left your Russia for good, poems sewn into my pillow
rushing towards my own training
to live with your lines
on a verge of a story set against itself.
To live with your lines, those where sails rise, waves
beat against the city's granite in each vowel,—
pages open by themselves, a quiet voice
speaks of suffering, of water.

❖

We come back to where we have committed a crime,
we don't come back to where we loved, you said;
your poems are wolves nourishing us with their milk.
I tried to imitate you for two years. It feels like burning
and singing about burning. I stand
as if someone spat at me.
You would be ashamed of these wooden lines,
how I don't imagine your death
but it is here, setting my hands on fire.

Joseph Brodsky

Joseph made his living by giving private lessons in everything from engineering to Greek. His eyes were sleepy and small, his face dominated by a huge mustache, like Nietszche's. He mumbled. Do you enjoy Brahms? I cannot hear you, I said. How about Chopin? I cannot hear you. Mozart? Bach? Beethoven? I am hard of hearing, could you repeat that please? You will have a great success in music, he said.

To meet him, I go back to the Leningrad of 1964. The streets are devilishly cold: we sit on the pavement, he begins abruptly (a dry laugh, a cigarette) to tell me the story of his life, his words change to icicles as we speak. I read them in the air.

Isaac Babel

What happiness is? Rembrandt, Petrarch
the servants of light
protected by geese, pines.

Isaac Babel knows: he invents a genre of silence,
a precise man whose silence lives
in the bodies
of others. A precise man,

a cigarette behind his ear, he drinks
with a Chief of Police and borrows money
from his mistress, writes lines—
difficult—there is fire between them.

He is making an account of his life,
I am still inside my body, he is praising
the dead: Gorki, Maupassant.
In moments of doubt
he drinks before their portraits.

What is happiness? a few stories
that have fooled censors. He won't carry
silence like a candlestick,
he will say to an ugly girl: *you are beautiful,*
you will walk above the earth at eye level.

Isaac Babel

There was no mythology: Odysseus hanged himself. Homer drank to death and stank of mud.

Isaac Babel knew. "I am a dance professor," he introduced himself. "I know different dances—polka and tango and flamenco, a dance of lust and of joy, of wife or no wife."

"Odessa is everywhere," he said. "But only Odessa can move her hips better than Odessa." He performed his dances barefoot so that he could "preserve the merchandise." When drunk, Isaac would stand on the pavement, calling for a taxi.

"Are you free?" he would ask, opening a door.

"Yes," a cabbie would say.

"Yes? Well get out of the car and go dancing!"

A tired man, when he laughed he seemed absolutely alone on Earth. As certain women passed on the street, he would turn and quietly say, "What a piece of bread she is, what a warm piece of bread."

"What do you think of Marina?" I asked him many times.

"I think she is a wonderful woman!"

"Really? She always says that you are an idiot."

"Well, perhaps we are both mistaken."

For years, my sealed lips kept the intoxicating story of his madness. As he delivered his jokes, I laughed with my lips tight together.

"Was Isaac drinking last night?" Marina asked.

"I'm not sure! But when he arrived, he asked for a mirror to see who came home."

Marina Tsvetaeva

In each line's strange syllable: she awakes
as a gull, torn
between heaven and earth.

I accept her, stand with her, face to face.
—in this dream: she wears her dress
like a sail, runs behind me, stopping

when I stop. She laughs
as a child speaking to herself:
 "soul = pain + everything else."

I bend clumsily at the knees
and I quarrel no more,
all I want is a human window

in a house whose roof is my life.

Marina Tsvetaeva

During the first year of my deafness, I saw her with a man. She wore a purple scarf knotted around her head. Half-dancing, she took his head between her hands and laid it on her breast. And she began to sing. I observed her with devouring attention. I imagined her voice smelling of oranges; I fell in love with her voice.

She was a woman who lived like a conspirator sending contradictory signals. "Do not eat the apple seeds," she threatened me, "Not the apple seeds. The branches will grow from your belly!" She touched my ear, fingering it.

I know nothing of her husband except for his fatal heart attack in a moving bus. There was no strain on her face, but looking at her, I understood the dignity of grief. Returning from his funeral, she took off her shoes and walked barefoot in the snow.

Praise

...but one day through the gate left half-open
there are yellow lemons shining at us
and in our empty breasts
these golden horns of sunlight
pour their songs.

—Montale

Praise

We were leaving Odessa in such a hurry that we forgot the suitcase filled with English dictionaries outside our apartment building. I came to America without a dictionary, but a few words did remain:

Forgetting: an animal of light. A small ship catches a wind and sails.

Past: figures coming to the water's edge, carrying lamps. Water is suspiciously cold. Many are standing on the shore, the youngest throwing hats in the air.

Sanity: a barrier separating me from madness is not a barrier, really. A huge aquarium filled with water weeds, turtles, and golden fish. I see flashes: movements, names inscribed on the foreheads.

A swift laugh: she leaned over, intrigued. I drank too fast.

Dead: entering our dreams, the dead become inanimate objects: branches, teacups, door-handles. I wake and wish I could carry this clarity with me.

Time, my twin, take me by the hand
through the streets of your city;
my days, your pigeons, are fighting for crumbs—

❖

A woman asks at night for a story with a happy ending.
I have none. A refugee,

I go home and become a ghost
searching the houses I lived in. They say—

the father of my father of his father of his father was a prince
who married a Jewish girl

against the Church's will and his father's will and
the father of his father. Losing all,

eager to lose: the estate, ships,
hiding this ring (his wedding ring), a ring

my father handed to my brother, then took. Handed,
then took, hastily. In a family album

we sit like the mannequins
of school children

whose destruction,
like a lecture is postponed.

Then my mother begins to dance, re-arranging
this dream. Her love

is difficult; loving her is simple as putting raspberries
in my mouth.

On my brother's head: not a single
gray hair, he is singing to his twelve-month-old son.

And my father is singing
to his six-year-old silence.

This is how we live on earth, a flock of sparrows.
The darkness, a magician, finds quarters

behind our ears. We don't know what life is,
who makes it, the reality is thick

with longing. We put it up to our lips
and drink.

❖

I believe in childhood, a native land of math exams
that return and do not return, I see—

the shore, the trees, a boy
running across the streets like a lost god;

the light falls, touching his shoulder.

Where memory, an old flautist,
plays in the rain and his dog sleeps, its tongue

half hanging out;
for twenty years between life and death

I have run through silence: *in 1993 I came to America.*

❖

America! I put the word on a page, it is my keyhole.
I watch the streets, the shops, the bicyclist, the oleanders.

I open the windows of an apartment
and say: I had masters once, they roared above me,

Who are we? Why are we here?
A lantern they carried still glitters in my sleep,

—in this dream: my father breathes
as if lighting a lamp over and over. The memory

is starting its old engine, it begins to move
and I think the trees are moving.

On the page's soiled corners
my teacher walks, composing a voice;

he rubs each word in his palms:
"hands learn from the soil and broken glass,

you cannot think a poem," he says,
"watch the light hardening into words."

❖

I was born in the city named after Odysseus
and I praise no nation—

to the rhythm of snow
an immigrant's clumsy phrases fall into speech.

But you asked
for a story with a happy ending. Your loneliness

played its lyre. I sat
on the floor, watching your lips.

Love, a one-legged bird
I bought for forty cents as a child, and released,

is coming back, my soul in reckless feathers.
O the language of birds

with no word for complaint!—
the balconies, the wind.

This is how, while darkness
drew my profile with its little finger,

I have learned to see past as Montale saw it,
the obscurer thoughts of God descending

among a child's drum beats,
over you, over me, over the lemon trees.

ACKNOWLEDGMENTS

Many thanks to the editors of the following publications: *Adirondack Review, American Literary Review, Born Magazine, Canary River Review, Chapiteau Press, DMQ Review, HazMat Review, Mars Hill Review, New Republic, Poems From the Heron Clan Anthology, PoetryMagazine.com, Pudding House Publications, Tikkun, Salmagundi, Southeast Review, Southwest Review, Sundress Publications* and *Web Del Sol*.

Some language in prose fragments in "Musica Humana" is taken from eye-witness accounts of I. Ehrenburg, L. Chukovsky, J. Brodsky, A. Akhmatova. "Musica Humana" is for Carolyn Forché, "Dancing In Odessa" is in memory of Eva Staroselskaya and Victor Kaminsky, "A Toast" is for Rachel Galvin, "A Farewell to Friends" is in memory of Charlie Bernstein, David Kadlec, Rex McGuinn, Marik Naroditsky, Anthony and Ginny Piccione, and Bernard Schuster. "Natalia" and all other love poems in this book are for Katie Farris.

I am grateful to The Poetry Foundation and *Poetry* magazine, Phillips Exeter Academy, the Milton Center, National Federation of State Poetry Societies, and Bucknell University's Stadler Center for Poetry, for awards and fellowships that supported the writing of these poems. Gracious thanks also to the English Departments of Georgetown University and the University of Rochester.

Endless gratitude to Eleanor Wilner for helping this book into the world. I am deeply thankful to Carolyn Forché for her help and friendship, from the very beginning. Heartfelt gratitude also to Anthony Hecht for his kindness and generosity. I am very thankful to Frank Bidart, Li-Young Lee, and Robert Pinsky for their inspiration and encouragement over the years. Grateful thanks also to Franz Wright for his friendship.

My gratitude to the following persons: John Felstiner, David Gewanter, Barbara Jordan, Robert Hass, William Heyen, Edward Hirsch, Cynthia Hogue, James Longenbach, Mark McMorris, Anthony Piccione, Jarold Ramsey, David St. John, Thom Ward, Affa Michael Weaver, and Adam Zagajewski, for their help with this manuscript at various stages: thank you.

I am also very indebted to friends for their support in the making of these poems: Ann Aspell, Jen Chang, Barbara Deakins, Maggie Dietz, Rachel Galvin, Garth Greenwell, Josh Kellar, Ruth Knaffo Setton, Rex McGuinn, Michael Odom, Charlie Pratt, Mary Rakow, Amy Ross, C.J. Sage, Jim Schley, Jane Schuster, Ralf Sneeden, Peter Streckfus, Susan Terris, Katie Towler, Alissa Valles, G.C. Waldrep: thank you.

Thanks also to Louise Glück for her kind advice in the final stages of this book's completion. Thanks to Joseph Parisi for awarding me the Ruth Lilly Fellowship and to Henry Taylor for the Milton Center Award, which provided much needed encouragement.

Thanks to Duff Axsom, Tipu Barber, Todd Beers, Robert and Peggy Boyers, Paloma Capanna, Norm Davis, Rachel Callaghan, Lynn Follet, Joan Houlihan, Larry Jaffe, Wendy Low, Margaret McGuinn, Michael Neff, Mark Ott, Nita Pettigrew, Colleen Royr, Harvey Shepard, Felicia Sullivan, Frank Wilson, Beth Woodcome, Marc Woodworth, Andrena Zawinski, for their presence in my life.

Thanks to Lydia Cherbina, Yurii Mikhailic and Valentin Moroz for the gift of Russian poetry in Odessa. And to Polina Barskova, Misha Gronus, Olga Meerson, and Valery Petrochenkov for keeping the circle whole:

Sincere thanks to Laura Halleran, Joan Bouthillier, Jane Shaffelton and most especially Gary Wiener for helping me to learn English language through writing and translation of its poetry.

I would also like to thank Carolyn, Harry and Sean Mattison for opening their home to me in a time of need. The Farris and Ajootian families for their warmth. Much thanks to Jeffrey Levine and Margaret Donovan of Tupelo Press for their support of this work.

And a special thanks to Katie Farris, who is present in every line. In Memoriam: Anthony Piccione. I beg forgiveness from everyone I may have overlooked.

Other books from Tupelo Press

Fasting for Ramadan: Notes from a Spiritual Practice, Kazim Ali
This Lamentable City, Polina Barskova,
          edited and introduced by Ilya Kaminsky
Circle's Apprentice, Dan Beachy-Quick
Stone Lyre: Poems of René Char, translated by Nancy Naomi Carlson
Atlas Hour, Carol Ann Davis
Sanderlings, Geri Doran
The Flight Cage, Rebecca Dunham
Have, Marc Gaba
Other Fugitives & Other Strangers, Rigoberto González
The Next Ancient World, Jennifer Michael Hecht
The Us, Joan Houlihan
Nothing Can Make Me Do This, David Huddle
A God in the House: Poets Talk About Faith,
          edited by Ilya Kaminsky and Katherine Towler
Manoleria, Daniel Khalastchi
Phyla of Joy, Karen An-hwei Lee
Lucky Fish, Aimee Nezhukumatathil
Intimate: An American Family Photo Album, Paisley Rekdal
The Beginning of the Fields, Angela Shaw
Cream of Kohlrabi: Stories, Floyd Skloot
The Forest of Sure Things, Megan Snyder-Camp
Babel's Moon, Brandon Som
Traffic with Macbeth, Larissa Szporluk
the lake has no saint, Stacey Waite
Dogged Hearts, Ellen Doré Watson
Narcissus, Cecilia Woloch
American Linden, Matthew Zapruder
Monkey Lightning, Martha Zweig

See our complete backlist at www.tupelopress.org